PEOPLE NOT THINGS

LOVE POEMS AND PAINTINGS FOR HUMANITY

GENESIS BE

Andrews McMeel
PUBLISHING®

Andrews McMeel Publishing
a division of Andrews McMeel Universal
1130 Walnut Street, Kansas City, Missouri 64106

www.andrewsmcmeel.com

23 24 25 26 27 TEN 10 9 8 7 6 5 4 3 2 1

ISBN: 978-1-5248-8481-9

Library of Congress Control Number: 2023935460

Editor: Danys Mares
Art Director: Julie Barnes
Designer: Tiffany Meairs
Production Editor: Brianna Westervelt
Production Manager: Julie Skalla

Cover Photograph by Ryann Jet

dedicated to my father, John Ellis Ishmael Be,
for teaching me the power of poetry;
and to humanity,
whom I loved before I knew you

Author's Note

My goal with my words is to bring human dignity to the forefront of our divided World. To advocate for compassion, vulnerability, and the burning need for freedom. Every word is born from unapologetic love and permission to be all of me, and as a nod to my inner child. With all her simplicity and complexity, I make space for the entire World. I believe in the good of humanity with all my heart though she has broken it many times. Consider this my small contribution, to move the unmovable, to tell the truth through hands clasped over ears, to nudge out what little space I can so that the next lover may thrive.

Barrier of Fear

A QUIET HOPE

A cavity in my heart
A quiet canyon I gaze upon
Not the type that travelers yearn to see
The gapin' space is my own to know
It holds a quiet hope

I'm too embarrassed to utter

I'm a lonely ronin, my sword inscribed with love
With no master to serve, she banished me
Perched atop a castle, I stare through the vast openness
I'm the only soul for miles
Uncertain of my journey
But my back is strong and straight
I hold a quiet hope
A warrior knows that fear is fleeting
To hesitate is to die

So I fill this cavity with a quiet hope
I'm too ashamed to utter
No other ear for miles

I could yell and none would hear
The light kisses the fog
As the sun rises to conquer the night
I'm startled to see just how vast
And ominous this canyon is
A heart that truly opens
Can fit the entire cosmos
Burdened with the pain of the World
Still I hold a childish hope

I'm too afraid to utter
Even to myself

Mercator Rejection

Sittin' in the musk of an old study
Smell of cigar seeped into fabric
Of chairs older than I
My little finger tracin'
The quadrants of an empire
On an antiquated Globe
Domains seem old as time
In my naive mind
This is the world I know
The world I'm learnin'
Each day
Perhaps it is human nature
Yearnin' for acquisition
Restlessness of the powerful
The clench of the rich

Leavin' pangs of empty bellies
Grief of broken mothers
The ominous blanket of lack
Entire continents reel from
The rape of their resources
And people
In their wake

This Globe seems off
Africa looks small
Europe looks larger

Benefits of mappin' out oppression
No matter the scale of deception
Indoctrination of youth
Who were never taught to

Question

Everything

A Trip to the Zoo

Aquariums and zoos
Remind me of prisons
Except people pay
To gawk at the prisoners

LEAP OF FAITH

Fear and ego coat the first step
Don't slip
The ones who coax you to dive
Into your destiny
Lead you onto the rising ledges
Of the unknown
Where faith in yourself is mandatory

Dedicated to Susan Davis

Assess the Exits

Double doors exit behind
Push to exit function
Single door entrance ahead
Pull to exit function
Women's bathroom
No windows no exit
Assume kitchen has back door
To an alley or trash

Every single room I enter
No matter how familiar
Or how jubilant
I assess the exits
I assess the demographic
A cautionary routine
You may or may not follow
Dependin' on how
Your privilege of safety strikes you
As I've been attacked
As a woman
Of color
Of queerness
Because my companion
Is gorgeous
Because my afro
Is bold
Because my swagger
Holds no apologies

In my Nation
Shooters mark bullets
For those they've never even met
And bullets are King here
Their reign is uncontested

So I enter the room
Radiant and poised
Ready to love and laugh
And eat and hear stories
But not before

I Assess The Exits

Morning in Timișoara

Buildings bleed old blood
Recite chants of revolution
Long live freedom
Slowly forming features of the faceless
My friend, those heels don't mesh with cobblestone
A River of strangers look then look longer
What a sight I must be
With my pretty face and baggy clothes
Kicks clean as Timișoara streets
I came here to breathe your wind
To smell your borscht

To learn the chants of revolution

The Old Red River

A little girl
From an ancient city
A city bordered by an old red river
A little girl was born
With no arms
To the townsfolk
She was cursed
A baby monster
She was banished
To the other side of the old red river
She lived there
With the other baby monsters
And with the adult monsters
Who grew strong
Out of pity
The townsfolk
Threw food across the way
Sustainin' the forsaken people
They needed them alive to say
"At least we are not like them
We are truly the blessed ones
Righteous in our actions"
The folklore says
"Anyone who touches the old red river
Will become like the monsters"
Who often drank from the old red river
The elders and the shamans
All said so
"Do not follow the river
It leads to Hades"
The origin of the river
Unknown
It predates the village
Content they were
In their ignorance
In their seclusion

They drank from another river
A blue one
Confined between the two rivers
The village fathers and mothers said
"Never drink from the old red river"
The little girl and her banished tribe
Delighted in their lives
Curious. Imaginative. Creative
They followed the old red river
Every day
Often returnin' to their mandate
With exotic fruits, new toys, and devices
The abled children across the river
Would stare with curiosity
As the little monsters played
And laughed
With joy unknown to the abled kids
The elders said
"These are the tools of the devil
Do not covet them"
Imprisoned by their own fear
And sense of superiority
One day
The blue river ran black
And all who drank from it died
Soon the village began to wither
The situation dire
The abled children began to move slowly
They heard a little sweet voice yell
From beyond the red river
"Brothers, sisters
Drink from the old red river
It will sustain you"
But the elders would not allow it
Before long all had perished in the village
Except one young boy
On the verge of death
The banished tribe again yelled

"Little boy, please
Drink from the old red river
It will sustain you"
The little boy's mind raced
With all the elders would say
Terrified of what would become of him
He approached the old red river
His little hands shook
As he struggled to unlearn
All he was taught
About the river
About the monsters
Who now stared at him with watery eyes
And deep love
The cold red water filled his little cupped hands
He drank the fresh clean red water
Just like that
He realized
There is no such thing
As monsters

Static

Flesh burns, the world turns
It never stops
Ripped skin, the world spins
It never stops
Wage war, it's paid for
It never stops
Young lives get confined
It never stops
Addicts to the status
Nothing matters
We're just matter
Nothing's tragic
Automatics
Young fanatics
Breakin' habits

No original thoughts exist
Regurgitated mindless chatter
Into an echo chamber
While your inaction suffocates us all
Typing away typing away tweetin' away
Congratulations
My condolences to the death of a generation
With featherweight convictions
With featherweight connections
And featherweight consciousness
Grass fed force fed
Grass fed force fed
Grass fed force fed
I will make you vomit everything that you promised me
Now a virtual virus
We're stuck in confinement
Alone with our thoughts
Becoming disgusted and violent

Asleep as a walkin' carcass
Putrid and passive
A wolf is a slave to her hunger
Her purpose defined by her needs
Weakness breeds weakness breeds weakness
Weakness begets weakness
Injected into the fetus
Your whole bloodline is speechless
Deaf mute and dumb as we praise the unsung
Toast to the immortal
Immune to the social
Feel the static
Our youth are obsessed with celebrity status
I feel that we're spiritually famished
In a year nothin' that you do

Will matter

Just go back to the static

MISSISSIPPI, THE MICROCOSM OF AMERICA

Mississippi is a microcosm of a Nation
Police exonerations and mass incarceration
Black and brown bodies
A commodity
Mothers separated from babies
Border policies
Quotin' Bibles & false prophecies
Our White House painted
With the Klan's ideology
Our leadership is exploitin' White Poverty
Keeping us separate and divided
Gay versus straight
White versus black
Based off fear
And far from the facts
Your supremacy is a lie
You accepted it
A confederate curse you inherited
Bigotry is blindin'
Your fear of the other
Has blocked your own blessings
From your sisters and brothers
Outrage fatigue
I'm screamin', "I Can't Breathe"
From the top it trickles down
From our Judges to Police
'Cause the illusion of freedom
Is far more dangerous
Than any jail cell or cramped cages

Yes, Mississippi is a microcosm of my Nation

Where cowards replace white sheets with fake avatars
Repeatin' their parents' folklore
Tooth Fairy Santa Claus
Where history's whitewashed
Google black codes and bylaws
In the comment section sound off!
Call me whatever you like
I been through worse in this fight
And the hatred in your words just proves that I'm right

'Cause Mississippi is a microcosm of a country
That always needed me but never wanted me
My melanin and skin is a sin
Sentenced to build your economy
Pack the prisons, fill the quota
Make us felons, never voters
Travel bans and deportations
Killer cops, no resignations

No federal indictments just mock trials

So my heart bleeds as the billboard reads
"Make America White Again"
As my favorite rapper concedes
Makin' me question everything that I believe
But still,

I have hope

Some choose to jump ship
And some steer the boat
See I know that love and humanity live
In the smile of every child
In the heart of every kid

So be brave enough to break the curse
We need you at the polls
Out in droves
Fightin' against the bigots you oppose
Study law, run for office
Make a call, write your congress
Use your voice, choose a march
Malcolm's gone, grab the torch
Read a book or write a rap
Just speak with truth and deal with facts

Alt-right affiliations
With federal administrations
Confederate infiltration
Neo-Nazis showin' faces
Just fuelin' the fear and hatred
While expandin' their corporations

Do you see now? . . . How

Mississippi is a microcosm of our Nation?

Exo Metro

The city is decaying
Collapsin'
Dilapidated
We couldn't care for it
Just like
We couldn't care for the land
Now scorched
It bears no fruit
All the farmers
Are dead
Corroded buildings
Stained by the poisonous air
We couldn't purify it
Just like
We couldn't purify ourselves
The ground
Is thirsty
Burns our feet
There's nothin' left
To take

RED DEATH

The fear of the unknown shadows us in life
Anxiety fades once the new thing is tried
Death of the body leads to
A kaleidoscope of possibilities
Beauty we cannot fathom

I've died a thousand times
And woke up to you

Every time

It's like seeing your friend in pain
Knowing there is nothing you can say
To take it all away
Drivin' for hours just sitting
Making space for tears to breathe air

Leave Me Be

Leave me be
Alone in my desolation
Keep not records of my triumphs
Or failures
Scatter my lonely ashes along gleamin' waters
Or bury my stagnant avatar to feed
The keepers of the Earth
Laugh from my pain
A necessary ticket
To ride the comedic waves of existence
My anxiety is not my own
Simply a consequence of a society's neurosis
A vacating of the bowels
From society's necrosis

Leave me be

But bottle my imagination and curious wonder
Between pale pages and audio waves

The only thing that is me

The only things worth passing on

City Limits

All hearts
Break fast
That's food for thought
My family only asks,
"Are you good or not?"
There's rage in her voice
As she's pullin' off
A million 'pologies
Never good enough
Sped by too fast
I couldn't grab her
That's a hard pill to swallow
The mornin' after
I'll burn the whole book
To ignore a chapter
My only regret
Is that I never asked her

Will you meet me?
Right outside of town
Will you meet me?
Once our spirits break free
Will you meet me?
Where crossroads lay silent
Will you meet me?

Woke up to the dew
On the mornin' petals
Her favorite kind of tea
And a blowin' kettle
Her voice in my ear
From another level
Her body that I touched
Through the mangled metal
Twin Flame name
Written plain on my skin

Wrong turn burn
Bursts flames from within
I can't rewind time
But sometimes I pretend
I finally realized
We never planned for the end

So . . .

Will you meet me?
Right outside of town
Will you meet me?
Once my spirit breaks free
Will you meet me?
Where crossroads lay silent
Will you meet me?

Barrier of Control

I AIN'T FREE

The illusion of Freedom
Is far more dangerous
Than jail cells & cramped cages
My tax dollars killed a child yesterday
I ain't free
Neither is she
My freedom is dependent
On the imprisonment of another
I ain't free
Neither is he

Lumpenproletariat

Purchase the rags
Assumin' them finest of cloths
Society
Followin' celebrity
Right off the cliff
To an untimely demise
The Emperor's new clothes are dirty rags
Ugly as hell
Rush to buy them
Scroungin' up the last dollar
A testament
To a declinin' intellect
An imprisoned mind
A failin' society
A Nation of followers
A willingness to be led
Right off the cliff
Of illusion and false gain
A middle-class man
Wants not rebellion
Lest his scraps be taken
His child stripped of the dirty rags
He blows his wages on
For his neighbor's approval
The weak are bound by chains of conformity
Comfortable in confinement
Look to those on the fringes of existence
Only those cast away
Can build a new castle
For their minds are outside the bounds
They know dirty rags when they see them
They wear theirs with pride and no illusion
Only the lowest rungs
Are immune to the trap
Of the follower mentality

Those who have a little
Want a lot
Those who have nothin'
And want not
Have it all
Have the key
To liberate us

Our Backs to Aleppo

Here in the West, we enjoy a good sale
Playin' with dogs and being glued to screens
We are unaware or disinterested in
The plight of others around the World
Aleppo, Syria, is one of the oldest
Continuously inhabited cities in the world
It now rots in decay from the recent siege
Thousands of civilians have been targeted and killed
We must never forget the siege of Aleppo
And the humans who perished

Collective Memory

There must be a response
To Trauma

I separate my identity
From it
Remember, remember
Like antibodies in a system
A resistance
So that it may never happen again
But alas our memory is feeble at best
New forms of slavery
Digestible servitude
Recycled from a past
We cannot remember
Left to rot in Books
We do not read
The new reality
On a phone screen
Delivered by nonexperts
Just enough followers
For me to trust the word
Thus continues the cycle of servitude

Another Refrain

If you think this is normal
God bless the insane
And their theories of change

The power of peace
In a chaotic brain
Isn't hard to explain

Weapons of war
When they're cold and they're stored
Are as dangerous as those
That are loaded and aimed

A child is taken
A child is born

Numb to the cycle of endless refrains
Numb to the cycle of endless refrains

Katrina

Young minds crumble from unfathomable sights
I know what I have seen
Coffins strewn about the highway
Boxed carcasses once loved
The mausoleum bare
And headstones pulled back into the ocean
My sister found her neighbor cold and gone
The rubble now sits about my demolished city
Citadels of ruin
Putrid smells unfamiliar to a young nose
Remnants of casinos cash coins currency
Thrown about the waters
Real life hidden treasures
Buried along the Mississippi Gulf Coast
My city is gone
Memories of places that held my childhood
Fade as the years pass but trauma lingers
She seized my thoughts and erased my memories
My adult mind riddled with holes in my timeline
Leavin' a hallowed belly in fear
Of the sound of rushin' water
Even the beauty of a crashing waterfall
Triggers terror, a sensation of being crushed
I'll never forget the sound
I hear voices in the melee
They've come to reclaim somethin' lost
Raging wind and bullets of water
Bombardin' my house
A noise so loud and ominous
I'm inside the throat of a livin' dragon
All remnants of control violently dash from my body
If this house stays intact it is by the grace
Of the Natural God

I awaken, all alone
In the center room of my empty house
Our attempt to board up windows in the face of a monster
Strikes me as comical as I assess damage to the structure
Pop and brothers ventured out to explore our new city
My mother stayed at the hospital to help the sick
Tales of lost livelihoods and loved ones, too
Sentences I never thought I'd hear
All my friends are gone but two or three
Most evacuated from the threat of death
We rode it out to bear witness
And we stayed to rebuild
We filled in a crater using pebbles of hope
Graffiti sprawled across neighbors' tattered houses
Declaring, "You Loot, We Shoot!"
I've seen anarchy with my own eyes
Roads shredded no way in or out
No police no firemen just survival
Starin' at the night's sky there are countless stars
No lights, no clean water

Time slows to a crawl, for weeks we stare at the sky
Waitin' for the sound of helicopters
We need help
I saw my community come together
For a brief time, race was irrelevant
Tradin' with neighbors
Batteries, diapers, canned food, bottled water
Birthed from the coastal waters of Africa
Gainin' momentum through the Middle Passage
Heated waters fuel the strength
Spirits surf the winds to reclaim dignity stolen

Forever etched in my young memory
The day I learned to truly respect nature

Access Denied

At the border we collide
Armed forces behind
Armed forces ahead
A Flag of white and red
Seekin' refuge
A twisted plot
My neighbor passes
But I cannot
Disbelief and panic
Coats the air
Let me in
Let me in
Please let me in

Leave it to a crisis
To separate the wicked
And the righteous
A war within a war
White supremacy at the core
Magnifying glass
Burning ants
Lookin' closer at circumstances
Melanated skin is a sin
In the eyes of Nationalists
Yes, the human race eats its own
Cannibalistic
No compassion just animalistic

But the greatest lessons
Don't live in books
They're in the stories never written
From the voices that are silenced

A grim reminder that it's up to us
To help us, to uplift us
To rebuild trust
The urgency
The rush
With pleadin' eyes I watch
As they look upon me with disgust
Sayin'

Access Denied

NATURE'S CALL

There are lessons if you watch my ways
Tides will rise and seasons change
Winter, summer, spring, and fall
The only law is Nature's call
Nurture Me, I'll keep providin'
Luscious clouds and Waves collidin'
Frolic in my forest greens
Cleansin' springs, endless streams
What was once a grand display
Now corroded, black and gray
We protect each other's lives
In order for us all to thrive
The branches that she climbs upon
The water she relies upon
We keep her calm, stars align
Change the course of space and time

FOR THE YOUNG GENIUSES

Here's my chance to observe my reflection
Studyin' a World disturbed and infected

A World that warps our perception
With no recollection
Of our Source

I neglect my intuition
To the point of no forgiveness
As young geniuses . . . we are livin'

On the fringes of existence

Face to the Light
Our feet on the Fire
Burnt Foundation
Holdin' up a Million voices of Doubt
Your ego destroys you more than they do
More than they can

When will you learn?
When will I?

Sobriety

Sittin' with discomfort
Chased by memories
I stop runnin' and call their bluff
Runnin' toward nostalgia
Difficult times
Facing my shame
Holdin' it tight
For a time
Anger exhausts itself
Into a rollin' calm
And every time I hold my shame
And enter an embarrassing moment
And relive every heartache
I set the table
And feed my feels
Nourish them
Welcome them
Speak to them
With compassion
Hospitality
After we eat
They do the dishes
They open the door
And leave

Until next time
Old friends

World of Wonder

Placed upon a painter's palette, all divided
Separate colors, all collided
Now we're bold and brightened
Despite the light that we're shinin'
The World around us is frightenin'
This darkness is blindin'
All this hatred and violence
There's a greater design
And we're all part of this picture
Let's invite everybody to become part of this vision
There's a spectrum we all live upon
Now there's a concept I can build upon!
If we can find a way to make the space
Find a way to celebrate
Then every soul can find its way
So lift him up and be his voice
Different faces, different places,
Different genders, different races,
Complicated is what we made it, Love is Basic
Celebrate it, Rainbows faded from the rain
We're just aimin' to maintain it
'Cause every color makes a World of wonder
And every piece is needed for the puzzle

THE BARLESS CELL

My love is such a prison that you cannot escape
Even though the door is open, you cannot find your way
Remainin' in this cell that you share with other inmates
Sharin' horror stories, never triumphs, only mistakes
I feed you now and then, just enough to keep you thick
I take from you to feed the beast, this cycle is very sick
From this cell, I have my picks
I take and return at will
You once escaped but could not replace
The way that I make you feel
It's better in this cell you say
The World is different to you now
I taught you light, then showed you darkness
Neither can you do without

They fed you empty compliments
Fake affection, his possession
But I shared your pain and gave you mine
I let you breathe, I kept you guessin'
There are no chains to hold you here
And that's what makes you stay
This beautiful pain & unbearable pleasure
Keeps you confused & drained
There is no lock, I have no key
To release you from this jail
So here you stay, forever and ever
Within this barless cell

The Curse of the Ivory Tower

In a white marble tower
Miles above the clouds
Lives a wealthy man
With talents unbound
He spends his days lookin' up
Then lookin' down
He looks side to side
But never straight
Every mirror in his home
He covers or breaks
When he looks down he sees the common folks
Mere specks to his foolish eye
He was once a speck who fought his way up
To the ranks of the rich in the sky
When the rich man looks up
He's surrounded by Ivory Towers
Much taller than his own
He couldn't grow past glass clouds
A fire of frustration grows
In the towers taller than his
Lives a people of purple hue
They stay in the towers, far from their people
Their purple subjects, they barely knew
The rich man looks side to side
Turnin' away all who question his "genius"
Surrounded by parasites
Whose intentions are fiendish
The fragile ego is slave to any who'll feed it
Regurgitatin' resentful rants
They nod in agreement
As the shock of his words go viral
They reap the rewards of his spiral

Stewin' in anger and arrogance
From his tower, the rich men yells out
"Hear ye hear ye my loyal little specks

Look at your pitiful life of poverty and regret!
It is the purple people who keep you there!
They're the reason for your troubles
The cause of your despair!"
His specks kill the purple people
Strikin' 'em down in the street
Except for the purple elite
Who live safely in their towers
Far from the commoners' reach
The rich man's plot failed to change
The taller towers still remained
He looks down in disgust
His people's weak blood runs through his veins
They are merely pawns in his struggle
For power and fame
A sacrifice for an ego
Unchecked and untamed
As his loyal parasites
Suck violently as he rants and complains
The press runs headlines
"The rich man is insane!"
Then offer him a soap box
To spew his disdain
Profitin' from the circus
They keep the people entertained
Fueled by the outrage
Conspiracies and false claims
If the rich man's insane
They do not care at all
Hand him a megaphone
Let him bare it all!
His giant frame covered in fleas
They grow stronger as he falls
Consumed by his own illusion
He begins to wither and withdraw
He isolates himself from his closest
Friends and family
Proximity to his people

Only mitigates his insanity
And holding up a mirror
Would only break the curse of vanity
His little specks watch a livin' legend
Rip himself apart savagely
He succumbs to the illusion of fame
The purple people's power never changed
Only the common folks felt the wrath
Of his violent rants and paranoid claims

And for the rest of his days,
An empty shell on a rickety throne
Obsessively staring up at towers
Forever taller than his own

Red Pills

Weak follow the weak
Sniffin' each other
Inhalin' the scent of false superiority
Circlin' misinformation
Momentum of confirmation bias
And conspiracy theory
Fake and failed intellectualism

No one reads books here

Consumin' heaps of propaganda
Never fact-checking or comparin' sources
Little men seek approval
And advice
From littler men
With big platforms
Dancin' in circles
Of misery and despair
Preyin' on young impressionable minds
Who've never known the love of a woman
Wallowin' in victimhood and self-pity
Disillusioned by the promise of entitlement
And power
For doing nothin'
Except being male
Or clingin' to the false identity
Of "white"
The stench of entitlement
Of being "male"

The inhalin' of the fumes
Becomes stronger and stronger
Until one breaks from the human centipede
In hopes of any ounce of attention
A break from obscure existence
Within a dusty bedroom

Daily routine of trollin' comment sections
The culmination of insignificance
Lost in arbitrary identity
Morality and code
Weak and unstable
Ever changing dependin' on who is speaking
Unable to stand on personal power
No clue of self-determination
A prison of self-exaggeration

Fire fanned by the flames of the rhetoric
Becomes an eruption of gunfire
Upon the innocent
Baskin' in their skewed morality
Faux Christianity
A red pill induced incel fantasy

Where men are meant to dominate
Whites were meant to subjugate
The principles upon which
A Nation was built
The myth of superiority
Shinin' an unbearable light
On his shortcomings
Lack of ability
Mediocrity
And missed opportunity of power
The strength of his ancestors
Traded for a chance to assimilate
To a fabricated culture

Assimilate to the ranks
False promises of inheritance

Unwillin' or unable to connect with
To cultivate

The beautiful spirit he harbors
The untapped talent he possesses
Choosin' instead
A desperate attempt
To leave any sort of mark
On this Earth

Can you recognize
The consequence
Of a warped society

In which we are all complicit

Sacred Domain

A chaotic explosion
Of conflicted emotions
Affections melt
Into hate and jealousy
Is it true love or manifestation
Of inner madness?
Elevated to the domain
Of the sacred

AUTUMN LEAVES

Autumn leaves don't die in vain
There's beauty in their pain
When I was a little child
Runnin' wild
They crumbled under my delicate touch
The empty branches were far too much
My sensitive eyes would fill with tears
Curious to why they had to die
The ground was covered by the bodies of the dead
Everything so gloomy and dark and red
It would be my first lesson in Death
My brothers and I would make huge piles of them
We'd climb up the tree and jump
Into the soft beds of death
Young life and laughter billow from beneath the bodies
Birthing joy, warm nostalgia, and memories of the smell
Of dusk and whatever Mama was cookin'
As the streetlights came on
Illuminatin' faint orange against the dim periwinkle sky

Autumn leaves don't die in vain
There's beauty in their pain

Mamie Till Taught Me

We deal with the same leeches
Rallies and hate speeches
Protestors go toe to toe
Bloodstained sneakers
This land of mine
Is in decline
Laws we can't abide by
The end of times
The hardest thing I tried to find
Was silver lining

A mother's love is a magnet
Like open caskets
Expose the actions of the savages
And evil tactics

I can't eat
Can't breathe
Can't sleep right

Built an army
I'm just waitin' on the green light

In this Nation
Nothing's sacred
Babies' lives bein' taken
'Nother body on the pavement
I need some ventilation

Till they apologize
Till they compromise
And admit to all the lies

I won't fail
I won't lose
This is the Life I Choose

And every time I put this pen to paper
I aim for Greatness
Never waiver in the face of fakeness
Passion of a fighter
Patience of a Freedom Rider

I plucked the Strange Fruit
And made a pie for you to digest

It's hard to swallow
We vote for men
Whose hearts are hollow
Shittin' on our past
Then promise us tomorrow
It's hard to follow
So I just lead forward
I need more
Than a dream or
Maybe Three-fourths
Of a keyboard?

Dayum!

Mistakes they can't admit
Lookin' at me like I can't exist
Feed me trash and bacon bits
I plead the fifth
Nothin' more to say

Till my dyin' day
I bear witness
I'll never turn away

I won't fail
I won't lose
This is the Life I Choose

BLIND

I cannot eat the pity that you have for me
I'll go so far as to say it doesn't exist
Only in your mind
Not mine
Strange how perception works, huh?
I was once a homeless man
I'll spare you the details of how
As I sat on a spit-stained sidewalk
A glamorous woman approached
She avoided eye contact with me
Her averted eyes told me
"You could hurt me, as any person could"
My heart responded
"You could help me, as any person could"
She stopped and we stood starin' at each other
For three seconds
But we never truly saw each other

For a soul that is at peace with itself
For a Spirit that is Whole
Seeds of division or hatred cannot grow
For that Spirit knows that there is no separation
No distinction
Between itself and nature
Itself and Source
Itself and any other human or animal
Or organism
I cannot see the wind
But I know it exists
Whether lightly blowin'
Or destroyin' my hometown
Its power does not depend on its visibility
I see you in all your darkness,
Simplicities
And complexities

I. See. You.

DARE TO DREAM

A million voices of doubt
Are piled upon my own
Who am I who dares to dream?
Who am I to believe things could be different for me?
That I deserve better?
That my people deserve better?
A million voices of doubt suffocate me
When I try to come up for air
To breathe the breath of relief
When I try to leave the heaviness
Of Monotony
The quicksands of Conformity
But who am I who dares to dream?
When my own history books teach me
More about my limitations and my trauma
Than my potential in life
The audacity to dream comes to us all
At different points in our journey
Either in waves of fury
Or gently like a pleadin' child
But who am I who dares to dream?
To touch a blue sky and add my own hue
To add my own color to the atmosphere
Who am I to meet the angels where they fly
And add my voice to their choir and their cries
I've dared to dream a million dreams
But need only act upon one
To act upon the voice of my inner child
Who scoffs at the word *can't*
Who screams back in the face of doubt
She runs away from the cages in which she's born
I need only act upon one dream
That cosmos may conspire to match my energy

Match my intensity
So I let go
I bent space and time
I met the stars on the dance floor of eternity
They've never seen moves like mine
I am the daughter of the unknown
The spark that dared to dream a brighter vision
I am the child of the infinite
Choosin' a human experience in order to test the limits
Of a system that predates me

A system that didn't make me
And cannot hold me
So I set fire to the old me
And stepped into my light
When they asked me, how dare you?
The audacity
I asked how dare you not?
Embrace the unknown with a fortified faith
Destroy the mirror that reflects the fear they teach you
How dare you not, wake up and rise from
The bed of mediocrity they have made for you
I once asked myself
Who am I who dares to dream?
I am me
I am you
Together we can dare to dream
A new dream
So big that our inner child
Says "I told you so"
A dream so pure
That all are welcome
And seen
Where no one ever asks
Who are you who dares to dream?

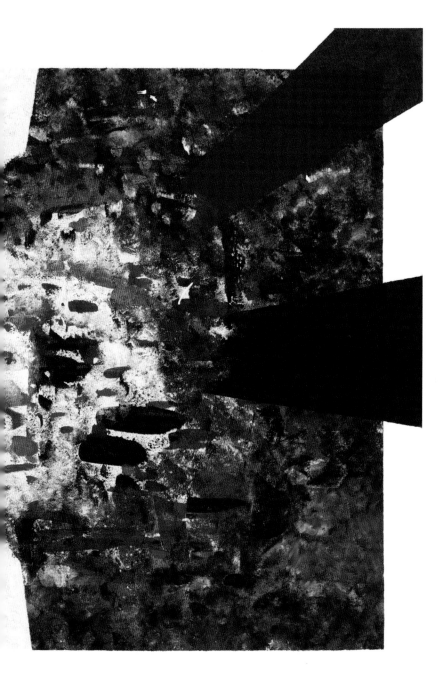

Rinse and Repeat

Popped out of a pipe
Frenzied and confused
Some lady shoved a hammer
In my infant hands
Welcome, we all work here
Earn your keep
The value of your life
A few bucks an hour
So I work hard
To build another pipe
Frenzied and confused
The alarm clock blares
Awakened from a deep sleep
Exhausted from the pipes
My tired eyes dart about
Searchin' for a break
Scarf down my cold lunch
Everyone smokes here
An excuse for more breaks
The whistle blows
I choke on half a puff
I run back
Popped out of a pipe

Barrier of
Communication

Activist for SALE!

Activist for SALE! A two-for-one deal
We love the idea of freedom
But not enough to make it real

God bless the paradox
Of bottled magic and brilliance bought
Counterculture, a rebel's thought
A price to pay when truth is sought

I write my soul
You write a check
Deliver my pain
You pay my rent

Like Banksy or Cobain
One is unknown
The other is fame
Only one is alive
To refute the claim
We cry for freedom
As we hand out chains

Tell the truth
Through deception
Of art
Whatever we protest
We perpetuate
Whatever we criticize
We make stronger

From Jesse to Sharpton
From Fanon to King
One's scope of impact
Is a subjective thing

The promise of change
The voice of the voiceless
Agreements are made
Revolution is pointless
None can avoid it
Not even the anointed

We lose our heads on the choppin' block
If we can't be sold on the auction block

Activist for SALE!

The Watchers

I'm screamin' PEACE
In the middle of a WAR

Like fallin' in LOVE
In the middle of Divorce

See digital outrage
Don't stop tanks
Removal of millions
Destroyer of lives

I'm screamin' PEACE
In the middle of a WAR

Black soot fills my lungs
Like hypocrisy kills the conscience
Young cries drown my voice
They say
"Already we are gone"
'Cause one life lost
Is far too many
Words on paper
Cannot hold PEACE
The treaty is falsified
The ink ain't even dry
So mute the mother's cry
Continue on with LIFE
Selective in your outrage
Obedient to the mob

I'm screamin' PEACE
In the middle of a WAR

Sendin' cosmic forces
To battle the four vultures
They leave us meager portions
While hoardin' the resources
Behold, the pale horses
Who ride into the horizon

And uncover the lies
As we strive to rebuild lives

The Industry of Division

So I think I'm gonna quit
I ain't happy here

Punch In – Punch Out
I check my timeline at the right time
Add my unwanted thoughts to the chorus of misery
Speaking only to those who agree with me
Passive-aggressive clapback
Against those who dare disagree
I suppose I'm just another worker bee
Helping to build the hive

I'm gonna grab a coffee, you want one?
Cream? Sugar?

They know that you and I will never bridge the divide
Or reach out with humility to connect or confide
That's what these cubicles are for
Anger festers behind keyboards and closed doors
Stuck in an office of distrust
Dishonesty, disgust

The fear they taught us keeps us employed here
Clock in, clock out
Bow down while they cash out
Too busy to reach out
Heart closed, head down
This is the new norm now
I think we've been worn down
By the Industry of Division

Communication creates an opportunity
To poke holes in the theories of bigotry through scrutiny
A chance for the truth to be told
A chance to educate and reactivate

So why do we refuse to communicate?

Instead we decide to elevate
Pundits and panelists
Political analysts
Each story more scandalous

They know what drives us
How to divide us

But I want to be brave
Not another slave
To the reinforced and repeated beliefs
Advertised on this webpage

And my carefully curated timeline
Between insanity and reality is a fine line
Don't want to sit on the sidelines
While my Nation eats itself alive
Inflatin' the prices of divine lives
Another statistic of bullets and ballistics
Somethin' twisted indignant
Using another's pigment
Gender or religion as ammunition

The alt-right and extreme left
Want SO much to be right
They're willin' to cause death

Republican versus Democrat
Fuelin' an inflammation because
There is an industry of division
Causin' addictions
Alcohol and prescriptions
Money from panels and keynotes
Talkin' heads driven by ego

Push that clickbait
Force-feedin' us sponsored ads
At a sickenin' rate
Pushin' false information
To the younger generation
There's no increase of compensation

This job ain't got no benefits

More likely to cancel another human
Than to reactivate them
Potentially collaborate with them

So how do you solve a division problem?
You must find the common denominator

We have more in common than we'd like to admit
We all want to be able to care for our sick
We all need basic shelter and sustenance
We all want to feel safe
From the police and our government
We all want our kids to have access to education
We all want to see the vision
That was promised by our Nation

I'm tired of tryin' to rip you apart
I want to speak with you
With an open mind, an open heart
We were all born with a spark
A pure light that we've dimmed
Before this world taught us to degrade her
Or to hate him

That light holds a Knowing
A Knowing that you are my brother, my sister, my sibling
A Knowing that your light is never worth dimming

This Knowing
I choose to fight for, maybe die for
Use my voice and my gift
To remind more
That the violence that they taught us
Was designed for
Commodifying our soul
Like products you buy in stores

There's an art to FREE THINKING
Let's regurgitate the Kool-Aid we've been drinkin'

Let's unplug from the constant propaganda cycle
Let's identify the bigotry in our history books and bibles

Let's go back to our adolescence
When things were simple and FREE
Let's clean off our glasses
So that the child in you
Can see the child in me

SEPARATE

Yearnin' for a closer connection
We turn to bottles
Social media
And false narratives of possession
We all just want a companion for this journey
A friend who knows us
But you are never alone
Forever connected with the web of creation
Separation is an illusion
Created from a point of reference
That does not exist
Breathe life into this very moment
You are Nothin'
You are Everything
But never alone

Slay the Night

We livin' good
We shinin' bright
We hold the fire
We slay the night
We gave our soul
We paid the price

So let them hate us
From afar
They aim at us
Like shootin' stars
Never changin'
Who we are

What do you think when it comes to me?
Where do you go when you run from me?
Will you be there when they come for me?
Do you realize what you've done to me?
I'm on a road and it's paved in gold
I'm gentle inside but they say I'm bold
I'm trying to balance
My multiple talents
I open my heart and they say it's closed

Oh well

All of my life
I tried to inspire
Inside I'm dyin'
I guess I'm a liar
My head to the sky
My feet to the fire
My only desire
Healing humanity
Raising it higher
I'll slaughter my purpose

The day I expire
That be the day
I'm no longer inspired
Weight of the World
Keepin' me tired
Prayin' to Juice
Prayin' to Peep
Give me the power to speak

Prayin' to Pac
Give me the courage
To Carry the torch
When they aim for my heart

Oh well

I built her a home and I waited there
A lump in my throat but I said it clear
She tasted the poison as soon as she kissed me
I took her spirit
Returned it with interest
I think it's simple
The fame and the money will kill you
Face all your issues
Handle addictions
God will not put you in any position
You cannot handle

All of my heroes
Have died from affliction
Killed by the pressure of fans
And ambition

I don't think anyone's listenin' . . . oh well

IDLE MIND

Disconnected from reality
Well . . .
What we are told is "real"
In a daze, let's drink
Focus hard on what's in front of me
Runnin' the wheel over and over
Day in day out
Punch in punch out
One day I'll buy a house and a pretty car
Nah
Today I'll dissect the Universe
Reconnect with the Whole from which I came
I'll challenge the stars and tell them stories of my own
I'll dance with the Angels and the Jinn
I'll ponder the sciences to create a map
I'll follow that map to the edge of Creation
My mind is Nothin'
My mind is Everything

THE GREATEST TEACHER

She is my greatest teacher
She taught me how to clean a skillet
How to place the salt
Taught me how mochi inexplicably tastes better
When cut into four pieces
She taught me a different way
To experience music and life
Through her sensitive soul & sad eyes
She is more than the colorful seashell she inhabits
She is the Universe all in One
She taught me true pain
And that no one is responsible for my feelings
Except I
She taught me that I love myself enough
To not take on her baggage
And as she fled
She led
Me back to myself
She taught me there is no "self"
With all illusions pulled back, suddenly

The grass is neither good nor bad
Every blade is right where it should be
She is right where she is supposed to be
And I
Have expanded the span of the Universe
I hold our sweetest moments within a clenched fist
The tighter I hold
The faster it slips through my fingers
Like sand
I know now, the past does not exist
Nor does the Future
If love is acceptance without fear
She taught me that fear was my lens
So I cleaned my glasses
Now I can see clearly

There is no separation between her and me
Between me and all of Creation

For what is heartbreak but a loud knock
On the door of awakening?

Dedicated to Nia B.

Mama, I'm Gonna Be Somebody

I'm gonna be somebody
Someday
When I'm a big adult
The little kids will point and say
"I want to be like her"
Regal and poised
Strong and bold
Soft and powerful

Mama ima be somebody
One day
The cameras will run to me
Capture my words and movements

Mama ima do drugs one day
Till I accept myself
I'll run through many lovers
Till I love myself

The harsh smoke will punch my lungs
It feels good to damage myself
A reminder of my fragility
My mortality
I'll make accessories of the most beautiful women
Until I rid my mind of patriarchal poisoning
I'll keep them around three at a time
Before I recognize my inherited insecurity
I'll keep around scapegoats one day, Mama
To blame them for why
I'm not accomplishin' my dreams
Not showing up
If it weren't for these false demons
I would be better
The weed, pills, the alcohol
I can numb myself

From pain that would otherwise
Make me move
Make me try
Make me inspired to change

Mama ima make you proud someday

Papa Said

Tender age of three
My papa sat me on his knee
He said "babygirl, tell me what you want to be"
I said

"I wanna teach the masses
My lyrics read aloud
In all the college classes
And maybe lead a revolution!"

He looked at me and laughed
Sat back
Took a sip from his glass
He said the destiny I chose
Was the loneliest path
Said I'll have a lot of lovers
But the love will never last

I'll have a lot of friends
But none that I can trust
You pay the price for greatness
With jealousy and lust

Never turn your back on those
Who wish you ill will
Assume everything is fake
Even if it feels real
Make a friend out of your enemy
Keep this in your memory
First you bring them close
Then you'll conquer them eventually

Patience is a virtue
A principle of power
It takes time to separate
A Queen from a coward

A Leader from a sycophant
You're born to be the former
They haven't made a bullet
That can penetrate your armor

The demons of celebrity
Are equipped and prepared
But Fame is an Illusion
Know yourself and be aware

Be careful
The path you chose
Is the loneliest road

Just let go

And flow

Where Source wants you to go

Stone Roses

A Rose doesn't grow
From regret and shame
It needs a lot of dirt
And a lot of rain

Put me in a glass
Put me on display
Cut me at the root
Let my blood drain

THE ANGRY ALCHEMIST

The older I became I understood
The systems under which
They dissolve us
I'm angry they tried to kill Leon
I'm angry that a puny man put the weight of the World
On Mr. Floyd's neck
I'm angry about what they did to my Big Daddy Clyde
To transform anger into purpose is alchemy
To transform anger into love was impossible
Until I did

Weeds

I can't see them or smell them
But I feel them
They steal our nutrients
Constrict our growth
This garden we've grown
Is vibrant and pure
But weeds are creepin' in
I cannot see them cannot touch them
But I feel
I cannot ask
For fear of being labeled
Insecure
After months, they've grown so big
I cannot deny them
Although I cannot see them
We live in their shadow
Finally I ask
"Who is he?"
I get on my knees
And pull pull pull
Pull it out of you
Harmless to you
But a promise was broken
Your word is your bond
As soon as it's spoken
So I burn down the garden
Weeds and all

When the smoke has settled
I ask
"Want to build a new garden?"

Yes

Then let's get therapy

The Search

Inside of me
Awaken what is dormant
Find that hidden place
Invisible to the World
And search for me there
I'm waitin'

THE POWER OF WE

The Supreme Reality behind the illusion
The illusion of wealth, lust, fame, fortune, and material
The Paternalistic image of God as an idol
The Father
Tear down the pseudo-truths and look within
WE are TRUTH
Chauvinism, Racism, Sexism . . . all the "isms"
Break down the barriers that have caged you
WE are FREE!

Can't you see?

Back of the Class

I was the kid in the back of the class
Asleep on the desk, drool on her hand
Writin' her rhymes pen and the pad
She tells them her dreams
All of them laugh
They don't understand
She doesn't give up
Devises a plan
She's makin' a scene
She's takin' a stand
She's stackin' her green
Chasin' her dreams
She enters the game
It's not what it seems
Studio time, she can't afford it
Men in the industry try to exploit her
When that doesn't work they ignore her
But her friends and her family support her
FBI files report on her
Media's lyin'
She's dodgin' the coroner

The daughter of freedom fighters
There's a fire inside of her
A warrior spirit is walkin' beside her
Spirit is calm with heart of a tiger
Her life is so lonely
With so many lovers
They just wanna love her right
But to her, it's just another night
Another city another flight
Maybe connect in another life
Shawty gon' miss her like summer nights
On the road
Fighting for others' rights
Takes a toll
But she is a woman that's on a mission

She doesn't question her own decisions
Do what she want without no one's permission
Blind to the cowards they blurring her vision

ashe

I was the kid in the back of the class
Asleep on the desk, drool on my hand
Writin' my rhymes
Pen and the pad
I tell them my dreams
And all of them laugh
They don't understand
Didn't give up
Devised me a plan
I'm causin' a scene
I'm takin' a stand

She found her therapy
In the bottom of bottles
She got too much trauma to deal with the drama
She follows the path of her father
She's far from a savage
Having a heart is a great disadvantage
She let it break
While she deal with damages
Keep it cool while they're panickin'
A militant mind of a strategist
Reekin' of cannabis
Tryin' to manifest
Dreams that we had as kids
We know that this hatred is cancerous
Dodging the wicked and ravenous

Lawd!

But still she knows
No blood No sweat No tears No growth
With a vest on her chest
And a clip-on load
Can't tell no more
Between friend and a foe

But I was the kid in the back of the class
Asleep on the desk, drool on my hand

Told them my dreams
All of them laughed

Barrier of Love

THE AMOROUS TRIBE

Old lovers greet new
Adoration, love makin',
That's worth fightin' for

LOVERS

And we'll face the darkness together, as lovers, as friends
Engaged in laughter, hand in hand
Using our words & smiles, we will make our mark
Our past riddled with holes
Yet our hands extended forward
You and I
Have work to do

The Gray House

I smell weed and incense
Every single day
In the gray house
Blue magic coats my hair
But cocoa butter breaks me out
My skin is dry and oily too
My curls are loose up front
Nappy in the kitchen
Mama loves beer and bratwurst
Our house is decorated with German mugs
Papa eats grapes and pecans
Not much else
We dwell in a modest house in Mississippi
Right on Biloxi beach
With my two brothers and our pit bull, Fatboy

As a family
We pray every Friday
A Muslim prayer
We also read the gospel and Torah
Every Sunday
We watch *The Simpsons*
And every day, we watch *Jeopardy!*
I always beat my brothers with the answers
They're older and stronger
But I am smart and observant
I follow them around
Learn from their mistakes
Papa shows his love with
Contemplative talks
With chess games and debates
He loves the Eagles and cowboy boots
Mama loves The Isley Brothers & California Love
Go figure
Mama gives gifts and cooks meals to fill our belly
Takes us shoppin'

Mama cooks soul food
Cornrows my hair every week
When I was born Big Mama told her
"You better learn how to braid"
And she did

My parents fight often
But I feel safe between the walls
Outside World confuses me
At least here, I am visible

The gray house was my trainin' ground
To express the complexities of my humanity
Of my womanhood
My queerness
My spirituality
My artistry
My family, my first critical audience
To build my muscle to navigate a labyrinth
Always so judgmental
But always loving
Willing to grow with me
And for me

Homesick

Something is wrong here
I don't belong here
I just keep paintin'
And writin' my songs here
Maybe she'll reach out to me
When I'm gone

Down in the dirt
And I'm done here

I cannot live for the clout
Money and the fame
Can't take away shame
Can't take away doubt

There's too much corruption
And I cannot function

I call my girl to tell her I love her
I'm leavin' tonight
I'm in search of another

Beloved

Why's it so hard to treat people with dignity
I wanna leave and just live in infinity
I need a World that can match my serenity

Lawd!

I know I'm not the only one
Who feels something is wrong
I know I'm not the only one
Who feels so far from home

One day they'll look back at my poetry
And finally know me
One day she'll look back at my letters
And finally see

Something ain't right
Why are they constantly dimmin' my light?
Put me in boxes
Label my life
She gay or she straight?
She black or she white?

But I'm made from the stars
A human the angels have carved out of flaws
Born in December
I'll die for the cause
Throw me on stages
With rounds of applause

Lawd!

Death and destruction
Fightin' and bickerin'
Everyone yellin'
Ain't nobody listenin'
There's no regard for the human condition
Our leaders betray us
Get paid in commission

Listen!

Why's it so hard to treat people with dignity
I wanna leave and just live in infinity
I need a World that can match my serenity

I know I'm not the only one
Who feels something is wrong
I know I'm not the only one
Who feels so far from home

DIVINE

The closest we will come to divinity
Your hand in mine
My mind a blank slate
Stuck in the state
Before I knew the World I know
Back when things were new
Simple and sweet

THE IMMORTAL MUSE

A Muse will never die
Immortalized in sacred waves
Her life and light conveyed
In every painting, every page
Every stroke and every note
Of every song I ever wrote
This cold wet dungeon echoes my thoughts
A circle of Vultures prepares to feed
On the corpse of every idea
That I've never dared to breathe
And then . . . there's you

With all your darkness and your splendor
Awaken my subconscious
With every word and every gesture
In your presence, I stay still
I absorb all I can
You delight my inner child
With every movement of your hand
There are parts of me you'll never see
'Cause that would make me real
The insecurities that drive me
The pain that I conceal

With every Muse I've ever had
A different part of me is freed
Enchanted lands I roam for miles
Witnessin' Beauty I cannot conceive
I approach a Forbidden Ocean
Exotic shells line its shore
Every shell is like your body
Harboring deep, a Divine source
I meet a piece of my Creator
When I see you, when we speak
She commands me to release my thoughts
To go find the strength I seek

You see . . . a Muse just cannot die
Immortalized in sacred waves
Her life and light conveyed
In every painting, every page.

FORT KNOX

Out of the norm, form
She is made from Granite
Ingrained. INSIDE
Society where she is . . .
Commodified
Possession is the Gawd
Love without ownership is Foreign
Unconditional love is Unknown
Most struggle to Understand
TRUE power is hidden deep within her stone
I saw her once, without her Mask
Her past and her pain Forgotten

Been blind since
From her gestation to her implantation
Follow closely as she grows
Soul sent to aid the child that creates the man

Nurture the seeds, without being poisoned
Such a demand
I saw her once . . . lately twice
No guards up, No walls up, No Fort Knox
A Master in disguise
So convincing . . . that she herself
Forgot her true form
Molded from granite

Ingrained

You and I

Imagine how high we could fly

If we wasn't at each other's throats
Shootin' down each other's hopes

Imagine how high we could fly

If we open up our minds
Try to understand the times

Imagine clear skies
And clean blocks
No need for cops
Patrollin' us like cattle
No death on our corners
Fresh food and laughter

No shackles
No cow-prods
No unnecessary laws
Classrooms filled
With revolutionary thoughts
Freedom in our eyes
No pointless nine-to-fives
Building our own lives
On our own land
On our own time
Our children are taught freedom
Of love, laughter, and life
Never taught hatred
Of how we choose to live our lives
Where we understand complexity
Where my brother stands next to me
Not behind me or ahead of me
My lover stands beside me
She ain't ahead of me or behind me

Our siblings are bonded by
Bullet holes and black steel
Children of the earth
Forced to forget what is real
Adapt to a World and A Way
We was never supposed to survive here
Let alone thrive here
But here we are
So dream with me
Let's love ourselves
So lovin' each other comes easily
Remember our past for the strength
We'll never return there
We are unique
The future we build relies
On our freedom of thought
Freedom from the poison of power & hate
We have become infected
Bitten by the serpent while trying to escape
I'll suck the poison from your wound
If you will do the same
We'll build this world together
Free of blame, free of shame

You and I, you and I, you and I

Imagine how high we could fly

If we wasn't at each other's throats
Shootin' down each other's hopes

Imagine how high we could fly

If we open up our minds
Try to understand the times

Imagine how high we could fly

HOT AMBITION

I set the night on fire
Just woke up to the ashes
Flying high on life
Until it crashes
Love notes scribbled sloppy
She will never see 'em
Probably couldn't even read 'em
My hieroglyphics are cryptic
To anyone who is listenin'
Love deep, fight hard
To preserve your vision

HOLDING PAWS

Her spirit is calm with the heart of a lion
Take my paw
The path ahead is a glorious one
I know you'll rise higher
The sun will come down to meet you
Sheddin' sheddin' sheddin' the weight
Take my paw if you need the reminder
Look within if you need a reminder
Feel how light this life can be

You are all you need

But take my paw if you lose balance
Floatin' floatin' floatin' up
I see more than fleeting beauty
Your season is changing
You adapt like you've been here before
What a sight you are
Your calm spirit unravelin' behind those pretty eyes
Loosening the knot and clearing your path
Glidin' glidin' glidin'

Her spirit is calm with the heart of a lion
But whenever you need, just take my paw

Dedicated to Ismahan

Kato the Potato

Dark fire embers glow in a forest of black
Starin' up at me with anticipation
With longing and instinctual wonder
Waggin' your entire body
You are a living lesson
Of the truest things in life
Moments that I've forgotten to be joyful and ready
Every small pleasure accumulates to the fullness of time
The white crest of your ancestors marks your feet, chest,
and chin
One leg propped up when you sit
No leashes for you when we venture into wilderness
Run free like I yearn to be
You run for miles there's no glimpse of you
Still you return to me
Every single time
My little black bullet barreling toward me
The less I control and confine you
The more you yearn to be by my side

Immortal (Leon's Poem)

Pursued my education
I ended up in debt
In pursuit of happiness
I ended up with less

I ain't trippin' though
My needs are always met
But quickly I forget
So it's tatted on my chest

My ancestors' test
I pass with flying colors
My Nation's up in flame
See the pain of crying mothers

My brother lives in fear
Try my best to lift him up
And love him while he's here
His ending could be near

My Mama's sheddin' tears
'Cause my Daddy likes to roam
And I'm my father's child
So my lovers come in droves
Tomorrow isn't promised
But my future is a throne
I bow to all my queens
Then I walk this path alone
The world is on my shoulders
My spine is lookin' crooked
I built my child's self-esteem
You broke her down and took it

And I know I don't look it
But I'm sensitive and fragile
I'm covered up with scars
The only armor for this battle

I killed a thousand pawns
Who reinforce the bonds of chattel
But couldn't reach the King
I'm up the creek without a paddle

Keep my fist tight
Every lyric hit right
Celebrate life
So every night's a lit night

I escaped the slaughter
I'm Mississippi's daughter
My energy is calmin'
But my rage is quite alarmin'

Like Government monopolies
Wickedness foreign policies
Made to benefit the rich
While killing us with poverty

I'm just speaking honestly
For those of you who can't
I'm spittin' real
Since most of these rappers ain't
You still degrading women
With images that you paint
But say you're for the people
Equivalent to a snake

We bonded by these bullet holes
Body full of lessons
That's how we eat our own young
Belly full of blessings

My boy should have died
So I'm basking in his presence
Saying "Breathe deep King.
They can never take your essence"

My girl stressin'
She watchin' as I die slow
She loves me with her eyes closed
Peeking through a blindfold

I'd rather die young
Than live a life with mind closed
Cover up my casket
With cheap liquor and five roses
One for every fear that I've conquered
For every ego I've demolished
And milestones I've accomplished
With this pen I'm a monster
To the system I'm a threat
To the elders I'm a champ
To these youngins I'm a vet

You are not alive
You are not alive
Until your spirit dies
Come out on the other side
Looking at my life
I might be immortalized
Even my enemies recognize I'm fortified

You are not alive
You are not alive
Until your spirit dies
Come out on the other side
Looking at my life
I might be immortalized
Even my enemies recognize I'm fortified

Love Drug

Trying to pull love from a drug
Wantin' the feelings to mean
That I'm being seen
And loved, held
Connected, enraptured
Caught in rapture
Cold burnin' pleasure
Lookin' into eyes that see me
For a moment
Then she looks away
Pulled from deep
Climaxin', cryin', sleep
Lookin' away
Being pulled in
Compelled, swarmed, by feelings
That I can't understand
Wantin' more
Fearin' why
Livin' in a moment
Wantin' to run from it
And toward it
Out the room and deep inside
Away
Wantin' more but knowin', fearin'
No, Knowing
There isn't
Or there might not be
Feelin' electricity from your fingers
Radiatin' down my spine
Pooling excitement
Anxiety in my chest
Swollen eyes
I know this isn't a need
I know this isn't love
But it's more than a want
More than just a feeling
More than a drug

Mutually
Seein', and takin' me in
Lovin' a feeling, to the feeling, giving in
Cravin' it, holdin' it, dancin' on the sea with it
Lookin' up, at you lookin' at me
Or past me
At a shadow in the distance
Are you here with me?
Am I, with you?

Or are we just on the same drug
Ridin' the high alone . . .

. . . Together

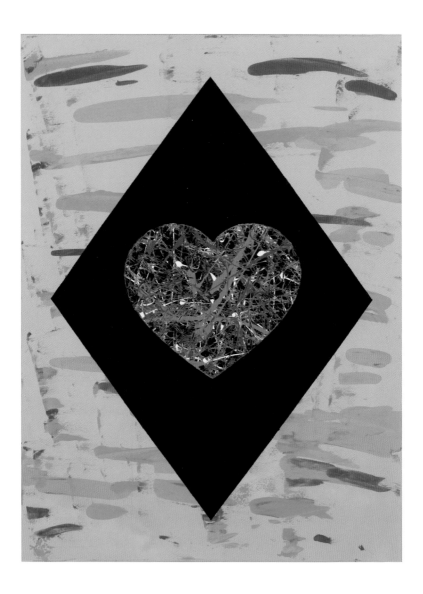

THE BOOK OF PARAMOURS

Climb your walls
Demolish mine
Lips to your palm
Trace our journey
Past pain never Dies
But I'll tell you it Does
So that I can come
Inside your Walls
I Crumble when you smile
The weight of your touch
Pushes me deep
Uncharted waters
Together we seek, a different way
To Love, to Live, to Let Go
My young heart knows the Mysteries
Some seek for a Lifetime
I'll show you, close your eyes
Fold your arms, block your heart from me
Feel my hands, so slow and guided

Feel my Lips
Heaven compressed to inches of flesh
Now open
Embrace me
Engage me
In a battle of lust
As we fight
Our pain combines, Crashes
Lashes Out at each other
I'll pull out all of your fears
And present them to you along with mine
We work, I'll work you, every inch of you
Until they wash away in the flood you provide
My paramour
Our moonlit adventures are fit for a storybook
Content am I, between your pages

Retwisting Your Locs

A pillow for that apple bum
Perfect as can be
Sit between my legs
And watch your favorite show
To know you is to touch every strand
Massage your scalp with oils
Your pothos plant watches our PDA
Sensual strokes of your perfect coils
Complexly wrapped like DNA
The foundation of life
My beautiful love
Let me save you a trip to the loctician
I gently shave your undercut
Save you a trip to the barber

A pillow for that apple bum
Perfect as can be
Sit between my legs
And watch your favorite show
To know you is to touch every strand

Dedicated to Nicole C.

Unreal

My right ear lays on your breast
My body weight on the rest of you
My hands grip your waist
I breathe you in
I listen to your body rhythms
To make sure you are real
Dreams gently pass
When our mind comes to rest
At times we grasp
Most times we forget
I freeze this moment
In a vault
Your voice resonates, reverberates
In the halls of every molecule
I take a deep breath and bask in the possibility
Multiple dimensions hold our longing
Across time and space
Our yearning
To snapshot this delicate pose

Dedicated to Nicole C.

Fierce Love

Inspired by Rev. Jacqueline Lewis

It's the gasp of fresh air
Caught between the waves of grief
The relief of hope
Knowin' it will leave
The trust you have in yourself
Knowin' pain will always return
Trustin' your ability to handle it
To know your despair
Is made weaker
With the gift
Of time

Fierce love

What is salvation?
Humanity don't need savin'
Only the foolish would attempt the impossible
An illogical task
There's no such thang
As spiritual evolution
The spirit is what it is
It's within, it's without
It's neither low nor a height to be aspired to
Then there's morality
What is morality other than another man's
List of dos and don'ts?
There's another kind of evolution
Another type of solution

It's the sincerity in my mother's eyes
When she tells me she is proud of me
It's the fresh froth from the espresso maker
I saved up diligently, to buy
Because I deserve it
It's the steadfast fondness of a child

Even when they mess up
And disappoint you
It's the faith that they will grow
It's facing that voice in your head
That nasty voice that says
You are undeserving, a procrastinator
Unworthy of the best in life

It's facing yourself head on
Looking at your reflection dead on
And bursting out into laughter or song

Life is alright

You will be

Alright

A fierce love weakens the low tide
It slows down the day
Illuminates the night
It's listening calmly and intently
As a man tells me why
My State Flag should harbor
A symbol of hate
It's offering him a glass of water
As we thoughtfully debate

It's when your beloved church burns to the ground
On your birthday
And you learn that celebration and mourning
Are actually rambunctious siblings
That do not negate each other
They pull from the

Exact
Same
Breath

An inhale an exhale
The spirit is within and without
Not a height to aspire to
Not a low to avoid
Just a balance that is brought about
By intentional, sustainable

Fierce love

If God prefers we do not take up idols
It's not because God is jealous or petty
It's because we often project power
Outside ourselves
As if the Godhead is not within
Like it's only without
Like there is a height we must aspire to reach
When we hold

All The Power

All the magic

We all are teachers of both magic and truth
Open your heart
You can learn the mysteries of the cosmos
In the great teacher of nature
In the great teacher of time
But fear can block your learnings
It's the lover that you'll always look back on with fondness
I clung to her so I lost her

Fierce love

I stick to what I know
But I grasp for what I don't
Constantly on the limb
Curiously testing the sturdiness of each thought

I move in such a way
That I aim to make her proud
Though she may never know me again

Fierce Love

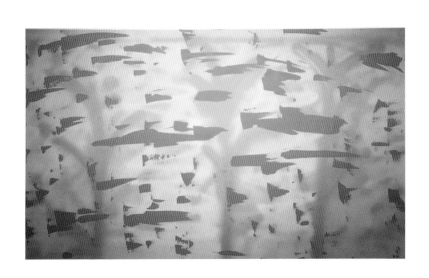

The Day She Danced for Me

That day
In Berlin
On Mary's couch
Feared that we may mark it
With our lovemaking
You wanted to make it up to me
A mediocre time in Berlin
But nights of poetry and shots
You have your ways
And your walls
But you wanted to
Make it up to me
"I don't want to watch TV . . .
I want to dance for you"
Your naked body I see
With a backdrop of all of Mary's
Travels and pictures
The energy in this space
Feels like rain
Outside a quiet cafe
After a rowdy night
"Put on any song you want"
And I do
And you move
Like I'm the only person in the world
My eyes transfixed
You are perfect
And
Move like water
Slidin' furniture across the floor
Bent over the chair
Your curves swirling
And slitherin'
I'll never forget
You slidin'
Dancin' on top of me

On Mary's couch
In Berlin

Dedicated to Nia C.

GENTLE

I need your touch to calm my chaotic mind
Your sultry voice to soothe my rising waters
Churnin' churnin' churnin'
They name me strong
But I am the weakest of them all
They name me solid
But I wear vulnerability like a weighted
Blanket
Comfort is raw and heavy
Your eyes seem lazy
When you want me the most
And my spirit will obey you
As you calm my chaotic mind
If you command me to control you
I offer you the darkest parts of me
I am the lover you cannot deny
Because you refuse to deny yourself
What you most deserve
Across the World I feel you

My imagination is as real as any reality
In my solitude I find you
Dancin' across the twilight's horizon
In your solitude
Meet me there

Dedicated to Nia C.

I died A thousand times
And woke up to you

Love Dies Slow

You made an impact
I can't articulate in text
Lessons you taught me
Like college intensives
The letters you gave me
I keep as momentum

The letter I gave you
You gave it back

I wish you had kept it
My heart was attached

I wish you could separate
Trauma from facts

Wherever you are
I'm wishin' you laughter and love
Your heart was the biggest
That I ever witnessed
I hope you protect it enough

Your superpower
Is sensitive
Don't ever let no one take it away
Or make you ashamed
It's part of your purpose
Like part of your name
We met with a smile
Remember that day?

The child in you
Saw the child in me
We decided to play
And got carried away

And I'll never be the same

Dedicated to Nia B.

COLLECTIVE EGO

Dependent on the other
To fuel our thirsty ego
Find a cause or an enemy
To deflect from the work
The work we need to do on ourselves
What do you love? What do you hate?
To love is to risk
But I must let love have its way
Get out of the way
There's immature infatuation
There's mature adoration
There's innocent adulation
There's quiet affection
And delicious confections
Poured from the ladle of love
Surrender your attachments
For fear and love cannot occupy the same heart

Trip to the Sun

I think this World
Is way too much for me
I think we should leave

Let's take a trip to the Sun
Don't know how long we'll be gone

You don't need no cash
Don't need no clothes
Just take my heart in hand
And don't let go
I stole these bricks of gold
To build this road
We're both poetic souls
Nomadic goals

This life that we live is an illusion
I'm dodgin' all these fakes
And this confusion
I know you have my back
I've got yours
So let go of your ego
Let it soar

Let's take a trip to the Sun
Don't know how long we'll be gone

Are you havin' fun yet?
We're chasin' the sunset
You don't need that blunt
You can throw out the cognac

My ex didn't know how to treat me
Promise me you'll never leave me
I need to hear you believe in me
My insecurities almost defeated me

They're dimmin' my light
I promise you
We can capture the sun
By the end of the night
When I'm alone
I speak with the angels
They give me advice

They say

"Leave all the death and destruction behind
All of the hate and the lies"
They told me go live in the sky
And follow the love and light

Let's take a trip to the Sun
Don't know how long we'll be gone

A LOVE POEM FOR HUMANITY

You are hard to love
You are hard to trust
But I love you and I trust
That you have a greater purpose
Than what you've shown
You broke my heart more than once
I was five years old
The very first time
Peekin' around the corner at the screen my papa was watching
I saw skinny men that looked like living ghosts
And little babies that slept as ashes
I saw for the first time how you eat yourself alive
Greed, possession, power, pain
Hatred, trauma, projection, blame
Still, the immensity of my love for you
Expands way beyond my understanding
That gleam in a curious child's eye
The slight smile right before you cry
So as to say, "Don't worry I'll be okay"
I feel like things are getting better
Try to convince myself that you are not as bad as the news says
As history shows
Besides, when it comes to you, negativity glows

With all your innovations
In medicine, engineering, technology
You have the ability to do better
Papa says be careful not to fall in love with potential
Love people for who they are
Not what you wish them to be
Same for you, I suppose